TECH TRACK™

BUILDING YOUR CAREER IN IT

BECOMING A
USER INTERFACE
AND
USER EXPERIENCE
ENGINEER

KERRY HINTON

Rosen
YA™

New York

Published in 2018 by The Rosen Publishing Group, Inc.
29 East 21st Street, New York, NY 10010

Copyright © 2018 by The Rosen Publishing Group, Inc.

First Edition

Library of Congress Cataloging-in-Publication Data

Names: Hinton, Kerry.
Title: Becoming a user interface and user experience engineer / Kerry Hinton.
Description: New York, NY : Rosen Publishing, 2018. | Series: Tech track: building your career in IT | Audience: Grades 7–12. | Includes bibliographical references and index.
Identifiers: ISBN 9781508175643 (library bound book)
Subjects: LCSH: Information technology—Vocational guidance—Juvenile literature. | Internet—Vocational guidance—Juvenile literature. | Computer science—Vocational guidance—Juvenile literature.
Classification: LCC T58.5 H56 2018 | DDC 004.023—dc23

Manufactured in China

Contents

INTRODUCTION

Do you have a favorite app? What is it? Why is it your favorite? Do you use it on a desktop computer, cell phone, or tablet? Is it easy and fun to use? What could make it better or easier? If you're interested in the answers to these questions, congratulations—you're a typical user of modern digital products who enjoys the wide variety of choices available. But if the "why" or "how" behind these questions seems interesting, you may want to explore the possibility of a career in user experience (UX) or user interface (UI) engineering. UX and UI engineers ask these questions every day. Their job is to make whatever project or product they're working on as enjoyable as possible for users. UX and UI engineers are part of a world known as information technology (IT), which involves the storage, presentation, and use of data.

Since the first product was manufactured and sold, customer satisfaction has been extremely important to running a successful business. Without it, a good product may not find a wide audience or enough funding to make it popular or even keep it in the marketplace. UX and UI are all about the user. No matter what a product's purpose may be, users must find it easy to use and enjoyable. This applies to almost anything we can imagine. Industrial designers of vacuum cleaners, kitchen appliances, watches, and automobiles must consider how their creations will be used and how users will react to them.

Since almost 70 percent of Americans use smartphones, computers, and tablets on a daily basis, UX and UI design has become an exciting field with many opportunities.

Joy Mangano, inventor of the Miracle Mop, knows the value of a user's experience and, as an entrepreneur, how important customer satisfaction is for running a successful business.

Although these terms are relatively new in the digital world, both UX and UI design have played a large part in the development of digital and non-digital products for over one hundred years. Even before people began to rely on digital tools to manage almost all aspects of their daily lives, user feedback has been important to both creators and manufacturers.

Today, UX and UI engineers have more tools than ever before that help them explore whether their products are fulfilling the needs of consumers. Using surveys and focus groups to monitor how apps and software are used,

It is important to give focus groups the means to test out apps and software on products if a UX and UI engineer expects to glean any valuable information from their opinions.

they are able to find what may not be working and tweak certain features to ensure the best possible experience for users.

Working as a UX or UI designer can be challenging. These fields require organization, teamwork, and knowledge from many different disciplines. Problem solving and communication are also necessary to succeed in this fast-paced world. As technology improves and advances, these challenges will continue to increase, and more knowledge may be required to take on bigger responsibilities.

These challenges are sizable, but the rewards can be great. UX and UI professionals are in very high demand today, and this trend doesn't show any sign of declining anytime soon. Above-average pay, great responsibility, and access to new and exciting tech tools make both UX and UI engineering fabulous professions for the future.

CHAPTER ONE

IT: A BRIEF OVERVIEW

UX and UI engineers work in the field of information technology (IT). IT involves using computers and the internet to store, retrieve, and send data, which is defined as "a collection of information." Depending on the purpose, data can be numbers, statistics, or measurements. It can be stored on hard drives, optical drives, and digital tapes, or in the cloud. A large set of data is called a database. Data is a part of almost everything we do that involves a saved history. Scientists use data to keep a record of their experiments. Doctors use it to develop medical histories for their patients. In the world of IT, data serves the same purpose. As a society, it allows us to see where we've been and what we've done, and decide if we should do it again.

Data collection is necessary in most scientific fields. Documenting prior research allows for both error correction and product improvement.

THE IMPORTANCE OF ORGANIZATION

Imagine someone wants to check out a book about outer space from the local library. Instead of having a card catalog to find the title, the head librarian shows her to a room with books stacked up to the ceiling. How long would it take to find the book? Definitely much longer than it should! Without some kind of organized structure in place, the library would be unable to know how many books it has, who has checked out which book, or even where the books are.

The same logic applies to data. It's the blood that flows through the veins of information technology. Unorganized data is virtually useless. It needs to be cataloged. Even if someone in the IT field is not working with data directly, his or her job most likely involves using, organizing, saving, or protecting it. The world of IT doesn't only deal with computers; these days, data can be sent through televisions and phones as well. Information technology touches almost every industry imaginable, including computer hardware and software, engineering, and sales.

Human-Computer Interaction

As the name suggests, human-computer interaction (HCI) is the study of how humans interact with computers and technology. Before the 1980s, the term wasn't used very much. Back then, very few homes had personal computers or any digital devices. Most computers were used by IT engineers or people who liked to tinker with electronics.

Computers were also much larger then. Some took up entire floors of office buildings and were run by teams of people. Additionally, many weren't even as powerful as the PCs in homes today. As computers became smaller and less expensive, they could be found in more households. Not everyone had the same technical background as the early computer pioneers, though. The new personal computers that were popping up in homes had to make sense to users who didn't know how to program or write code.

(Continued on the next page)

(Continued from the previous page)

The operating system of the first Apple Macintosh marked the beginning of a new age in human-computer interaction (HCI), which put more focus on user interfaces.

People were curious and excited about the possibilities personal computers offered. New operating systems and user interfaces were developed to help people interact with the machines of the PC age. Instead of presenting only a blinking cursor upon startup, new home PCs had text menus. As technology advanced, new interfaces used images, graphic menus, and icons that could be chosen by using a keyboard or mouse. This new type of graphical user interface (GUI) helped change the world. GUI allowed people to interact with their computers to do homework, balance budgets, and play games.

The key to the popularity of these early PCs was usability. Making computers user-friendly and easier to understand is the core of HCI. Today, human-computer interaction is a consideration for more than just desktop computers. It covers the way we interact with the GUIs of our cell phones, televisions, ATMs, and more.

Managing Data Is a Big Job

User interface and user experience engineers are part of the IT field, but there are many other people working at different tasks to ensure the efficient and productive use of data. The amount of data traveling along the information superhighway is huge. Big data can't be managed by just a few highly focused engineers; many other highly skilled workers are needed to make this possible.

Data engineers build the systems and software that organize piles of data into easy-to-access databases. Much of their work is behind the scenes, but it forms the backbone of database technology. Data engineers often maintain the systems they design for the most efficient flow of data. Many data engineers work with "big data"—sets of information so large and complex that they couldn't possibly be managed by humans. Data engineers normally have a strong background in computer programming.

Database administrators use software to make sure that databases designed by data engineers are healthy. They gather, manage, and store data and prepare it for sharing within a company or with other organizations. They also make sure that saved data is continually backed up. Database administrators keep databases secure against outside threats and data corruption.

Software engineers help design and develop the programs and operating systems that make computers run. They know how to program and code and are often

involved in many of the steps leading up to and follow-
ing the creation of software as well. This includes testing
for problems, maintaining the software, fixing problems
as they come up, and constantly working to improve how
these programs and systems work for users. Software
engineers must have a strong background in computer
science, math, and engineering.

Data needs to be shared and distributed. This is where
system administrators enter the picture. They develop,
install, and maintain all of the computer networks for
companies and other organizations. The scope of their
work is wide and includes working with servers, desktop
computers, mobile devices, and email. In many cases,

Data management is a large field that
requires many specialized skills. Keeping
track of information and data is a major
concern for many types of businesses today.

system administrators physically repair equipment and train other employees on its use. Without systems administrators, networked communication would grind to a halt.

Systems analysts bridge the different worlds of business and IT. Technical analysts look at computer systems to see if they really suit a company's needs. They work with nontechnical management to figure out how computer systems and IT will help businesses achieve their goals. This can include analyzing costs, designing specific software and hardware, and making improvements on systems that are already in place.

Project managers have a lot of responsibility. All other IT jobs discussed so far report to a technical project manager at some point. Project managers plan, schedule, and oversee the work of data engineers, software engineers, technical analysts, and many other IT employees in an organization. Depending on the company and their specific job title, technical project managers may work on one specific project or be responsible for multiple projects at the same time.

Quality assurance engineers look for flaws. They test and analyze software, find errors, and fix them before they create problems for customers or users. They plan and schedule tests, keep data on those tests, and fix bugs and errors as they are detected.

There are two more IT careers to discuss: user interface (UI) and user experience (UX) engineers. The remainder of this book will explore these two interesting professions.

CHAPTER TWO

USER EXPERIENCE AND USER INTERFACE: THE WIDE VIEW

If you decide to surf the web for additional research after reading this book, be prepared to come across a few different terms for user interface and user experience engineers. Depending on who is hiring, companies may advertise for UX/UI "engineers," "researchers," "designers," or "professionals." Looking at the big picture, all of the terms mentioned are included in the wide view of these professions.

Different companies have different views of what they define UX and UI to be. Companies with larger staffs often split responsibilities between staffers, while in smaller organizations, a UX designer and engineer might be the same person. In this book, "engineer" and "designer" will be used interchangeably.

UX: THE BIG UMBRELLA

UX and UI engineers are often found working together, but in many cases, neither one could do the other's job on a particular project. It may help to imagine the job of a UX engineer as a large umbrella. Like the mechanical parts that give an umbrella its shape, user experience design deals with the overall structure of an app or website. A UX engineer can be responsible for some or all of them depending on the project. They include:

- » **Interaction design:** The interaction (the way things relate to one another) between a user and the screen.
- » **Information architecture:** The structure and organization of a website or app and the way a user moves through it.
- » **Functionality:** Whether a piece of software or an app does what it's supposed to.
- » **User interface:** How a user interacts with a computer or device.
- » **Usability:** How easy a user interface is to use.
- » **Content strategy:** Planning for the creation, management and updating of the content (the words and images a user sees).
- » **Typography:** The organization and style of fonts and typefaces in digital and print media.
- » **Visual design:** The way colors, typography, and images are organized and presented to a user; sometimes called graphic design.

User experience designers must be able to make a product work smoothly across multiple platforms and devices.

This list above also shows us how much responsibility is involved in user experience. Although the final product is used on digital devices, many UX engineers rarely program or code. That job is usually taken on by front-end designers who build the websites and applications. UX designers work to give customers and users the most satisfying experience possible.

Although knowing how to code is not necessary to this career, it's never a bad skill to have. Knowing the nuts and bolts behind apps and developer tools can help create a great working relationship between UX professionals and front-end designers.

The less work users feel like they are doing to accomplish a task on a website or application, the more satisfied they'll be. Unfortunately, this can sometimes mean that really good UX work may not get the attention it deserves.

While it is important for UX engineers to improve bad products and bad features, they are constantly working to improve apps or features that are already working well. Having one or several successful products doesn't give that company license to relax.

USABILITY: THE USER IS KING

UX engineers provide clear communication between developers and users. On one side, they have to meet the goals of their employers. On the other, they need to oversee a project that users will like, enjoy, and, most importantly, use.

Meeting the needs of both client and user requires balance. One of the best measures of success is usability. Of course, the other responsibilities of UX are very important, but if a product is not exciting or engaging, users will probably abandon it.

The definition of "usability" is easy to understand: "how a user interacts with a computer or device." But beneath the surface, there are questions that UX designers should be asking that can make a design really

Marcus Vitruvius Pollio and the Roots of UX

One of the first people to design with the user in mind was first-century BCE architect Marcus Vitruvius Pollio (90 BCE–20 BCE). As Julius Caesar's chief architect, he traveled throughout the Roman Empire and saw how different cultures approached design. Vitruvius was also an expert in military strategy, and he designed weapons as well as churches.

Vitruvius looked to the past for his ideas. He was inspired by the great structures of ancient Greece, built hundreds of years before his birth. In his mind, a broad knowledge was needed to achieve great design. With this in mind, he wrote a ten-volume series called *On Architecture.* Each book in the series focused on different subjects that were related to architecture at that time, including astronomy. These books influenced architecture, engineering, and design for the next 1,500 years.

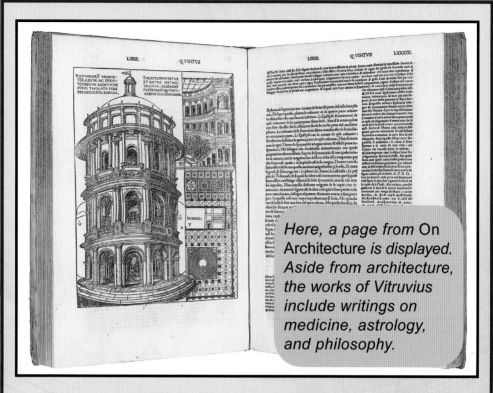

Here, a page from On Architecture *is displayed. Aside from architecture, the works of Vitruvius include writings on medicine, astrology, and philosophy.*

Vitruvius didn't see the point of building something that didn't serve a purpose. When he designed, he always had three goals in mind, which are now known as the Three Principles of Architecture:

» **_Firmitas_ (Durability):** An item should last long and stay in usable condition.

» **_Utilities_ (Function):** An item should always work well for users.

» **_Venustatis_ (Beauty):** An item should be enjoyable and provide delight to users.

These principles could be a guideline for UX and UI designers today.

successful and enjoyable for users. The Nielsen Norman Group, one of the oldest UX consulting firms, outlines them as such:

- » **Learnability:** How long do users need to figure out basic tasks on first use?
- » **Efficiency:** How quickly can tasks be performed?
- » **Memorability:** If a person doesn't use an app or device for some time, how quickly can he or she pick it back up?
- » **Errors:** If mistakes are made, can they be fixed easily?
- » **Satisfaction:** How enjoyable is using it?

Usability is only one part of the UX umbrella. But

Good user interface should make it as easy as possible for a user to complete a wide variety of tasks without frustration.

remember, each piece of the umbrella needs to work well in order for the entire project or design to be successful. A lack of attention to any one or more of these may mean a failure to capture user support and interest.

UI: NOT JUST SUPPORT

Noted computer scientist Ben Schneiderman was once quoted as saying, "A picture is worth a thousand words. An interface is worth a thousand pictures." While UX engineers are concerned with overall customer satisfaction, UI engineers are even more focused on the user. User interface designers are responsible for any and every way a user can interact with a device. This includes everything from screens and displays to help messages and login screens.

UI design involves working both on and below the surface. Appearance is extremely important in UI design. The way a site or app looks can make a huge difference when it comes to attracting users. Going below the surface matters, too. They must consider the number of steps users have to take, the amount of response time users have when selecting their choice, and other factors when designing a device.

Specializing in user interfaces requires an awareness of each and every interaction a user may have with a digital device. Attention to detail is so necessary to this profession. Considering the dozens, hundreds, or even thousands of interactions a user may have takes patience, as well as a back-to-front knowledge of what an app or device can do. Think again of a UX umbrella. Interaction design, information architecture, and visual design are all included within it. These jobs form a large part of a UI designer's responsibilities.

Not all UX engineers can perform the specific work of UI designers, but it's important for them to know as much as possible about what UI involves. UX design has so many moving parts and responsibilities that it's difficult to be an expert in every phase of the work that leads up to a finished product. This can be extremely helpful when setting deadlines and making adjustments.

Like the many different systems inside a car, UX and UI designers work together to anticipate and satisfy a user's needs.

COMPARING UX AND UI

As mentioned before, UX and UI are essential to one other. Any project that neglects one of these design strategies is not very likely to be successful or give users a satisfying experience. Rahul Varshney, founder of Foster.com, describes the difference like this: "A User Interface (UI) without User Experience (UX) is like a painter slapping paint onto a canvas without thought; while UX without UI is like the frame of a sculpture with no papier mâché on it."

Another way to highlight the difference between these two fields is using the analogy of a car. UX is similar to what happens when driving a car. Everything else—the stereo, steering wheel, and tires, for example—falls into the realm of UI.

A UX engineer could see a project to its end without a UI designer, but that would often result in weaker experiences for users. Often, it's very difficult for a UX engineer to get involved in the smaller details that are the concern of UI professionals.

CHAPTER THREE

WELCOME TO THE DIGITAL AGE

To fully understand what UX and UI are today, a person should take a look at the path leading up to this point. Much of the work UX and UI designers do has its basis in the early days of networking, which resulted in the largest computer network in the world: the internet.

NETWORKING AND THE INTERNET

Networking occurs when computers with different servers communicate with one other. The internet is a network of networks—linked computers and servers that can send and receive data between one another.

The internet began in 1969 with a communications network called Advanced Research Projects Agency Network (ARPANET). It was originally used as a communication tool for the military during wartime. Later, a set of networking rules called TCP/IP was developed. If the internet is a series of highways, then TCP/IP are the rules of the road for navigating it. At first, colleges and universities used this network for file sharing and emailing, and it proved to be a great way to exchange information. The possibilities were incredible, though the technology still needed to catch up.

HOW THE WORLD WIDE WEB CHANGED EVERYTHING

By the late 1970s, smaller and cheaper personal computers began to make their way into people's homes. The owners of these new computer were not all hackers or programmers, and as such they wanted different things from their computer systems than previous consumers. Studying the variety of ways in which new users were interacting with their computers became much more important for the success of computer design.

By 1989, one in every six American homes had a personal computer. That same year, a British computer scientist named Tim Berners-Lee wrote the code that is the basis of the World Wide Web as we know it today. Three major aspects of the code that users interact with daily are:

» **HTML (hypertext markup language).** This is the language that gives web pages their structure. It basically tells your web browser how to display files and information that it locates. This display is called a web page.

» **URI (uniform resource identifier).** Better known as a URL, a URI is a unique address that every website has. The "resource" portion of the name is the web address of a particular site.

» **HTTP (hypertext transfer protocol).** Better known as links or hyperlinks, HTTP lets users click on icons, pictures, and highlighted links to access documents on other websites.

Although the terms are used interchangeably, the "internet" and the "World Wide Web" (more commonly referred to as simply "the web") are not the same. The internet is a network of networks all around the world, while the web is made up of linked pages that are accessed through the internet.

THE DAWN OF THE BROWSER

Berners-Lee also wrote code for the first web browser, which let users both create and browse web pages. As the web browser continued to develop, a real need for engaging user experiences emerged.

The browsers of the early 1990s were much less complex than those of today. Most early web pages were static. The data browsers obtained from websites could not be changed except by web developers or programmers. Today, many websites are still static if they're only displaying information such as business hours.

The release of Mosaic in 1993 was a major step. This browser had traces of the powerful browsers used today, including bookmarks, web history, and sound. The launch of Netscape Navigator in 1995 took these advances even further. Before Netscape, users couldn't see a web page until all of the data was downloaded. Before high-speed internet, this could take minutes instead of seconds. The arrival of Navigator was a huge step for user interfaces.

During the next few years, coding made browsers more dynamic. Search suggestions, close buttons, and updates all came into being during this time. Users could have a different experience every time they accessed a web page and input information with a keyboard, mouse, or other input tool.

UX AND THE EARLY WEB

In the 1990s, the terms "UX" or "UI" didn't exist as they do today. Back then, the people who created and maintained websites were called webmasters. They were also sometimes expected to write code and perform maintenance and repair on hardware. They were project managers, skilled coders, and more.

Many of the webmasters' responsibilities have become separate jobs today. The work of today's front-end developers, systems administrators, and web designers was at one time all accomplished by one or two people. Some former webmasters have made the transition to careers in UX and UI.

The Xerox Alto II and other early computers of the 1970s were instrumental in the development of modern computers and other digital devices.

UI AND THE EARLY WEB

Many early computers were designed for experts. Most of them didn't have any interactive graphics. Users were presented with a blinking cursor and a few menus. The first real graphical user interface (GUI) was developed by Xerox in the 1970s. The Alto Workstation introduced the world to the desktop, icons, and application windows.

This was the birth of modern user interface design. The Alto wasn't even designed for consumers; it was created for in-house employee use and university research. Despite the intent, the Alto was designed to be both functional and easy to use.

The demand for UI wasn't high in the early days of the web, either. Since web pages were static and read-only, graphic design was sufficient for web pages. Data could be accessed and read, but user interaction was still minimal. GUIs became more plentiful and complex during the 1980s. Display screens added colors, higher resolution, and icons, making user interaction more enjoyable. Once programmers and engineers saw what was possible with GUIs, progress quickened.

THE DIGITAL AGE: WEB 2.0

The next big advance in UX and UI came in the early 2000s with the development of Web 2.0, which made the

World Wide Web much more interactive. Web software such as Flash and Java created new ways for users to interact with web pages. These new complex interactions increased the need for UX and UI designers. Websites became dynamic, and users gained the ability to generate their own content. This was made clear by sites like Wikipedia, a free online encyclopedia written by millions of contributors. Wireless networks were an important part of this development. They enabled folks to communicate almost instantly through Facebook, blogs, and forums. Faster processing power was necessary to complete the picture, and it allowed Web 2.0 to blossom.

Bad UX

Since the best UX is "invisible," bad user experiences are much easier to detect than good ones. Sometimes, though, bad UX must remain in place until a solution is found and implemented. Here are a few examples of less-than-perfect UX experiences that most people have experienced and must tolerate until they're fixed in the future.

Phone locks: The ability to lock our phones is extremely useful. Keeping personal information secure in case our phones are lost or stolen is great, but users don't necessarily feel a sense of joy when phone locks activate. If a phone locks during a call, it has to be manually unlocked in order for the user to hang up, mute a call, or activate the speakerphone.

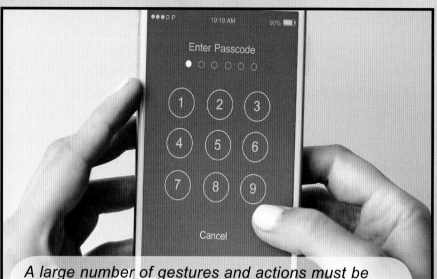

A large number of gestures and actions must be considered when designing for a user. Features that interfere with UX quality can be corrected through updates or new user interfaces.

Bad transitions: Some desktop websites are great to use, but the corresponding mobile version or app is not. Sometimes, they don't duplicate the same experience across multiple platforms. Some features may be missing, or an app may involve added features that aren't available on the desktop version.

Small buttons: Although fingers make great tools for navigation of smartphone apps, not all fingers are the same size. People with bigger hands often have trouble hitting the letters they'd like to on mobile apps.

These are the types of issues that UX and UI designers consider. Finding and analyzing bad UX gives them the opportunity to eliminate those mistakes in their own work.

THE SMARTPHONE COMES TO TOWN

The next advance in GUI, the touchscreen, reached worldwide recognition with the release of the iPhone in 2007. The iPhone wasn't the first mobile device—personal digital assistants (PDAs) had been around since the 1990s—but the user interface was revolutionary. First, it replaced styluses and buttons with one of the simplest tools of all: the human finger. With a series of movements, users could now tap, pinch, and swipe the same way every time on different applications. The biggest advance,

Modern touchscreen technology was invented in the 1970s but did not become a part of everyday life until the twenty-first century.

however, was the touchscreen. It was much more respon-sive than previous screens in use at ATMs and airports. And each application looked like Apple had made it, even if it had been developed by another company. In other words, the apps fit into the world of the phone to create a seamless, almost invisible, user experience.

Smartphones moved interactivity out of the browser. Nowadays, desktops, smart televisions, and other appliances all use apps. In addition to designing across browsers, as well as different screen sizes and resolutions, modern UX and UI engineers have to consider phones, tablets, tele-visions, kiosks, and other platforms. The smartphone era created a bright and busy future for UX and UI design.

CHAPTER FOUR

UX ENGINEERS: THE JOB

Although some companies combine UX and UI into one role, each position has a distinct and clear set of responsibilities. UX engineers are responsible for research and development, design, building, and integrating products. They are also responsible for improvements and fixes after the product is launched.

PHASE ONE: INITIAL RESEARCH AND DEVELOPMENT

The first step for UX designers is research. Coming up with a good strategy can define an entire project and sometimes an entire company. Since there are so many people and jobs involved, planning is essential. Research is also a chance for the engineer to put himself or herself into a user's shoes and discover a target audience.

An initial design step would be to look at other apps and websites to see how they approach similar projects. Competitive research lets UX engineers see what other companies are doing well and doing poorly.

Human behavior plays a big part in the development process. UX designers often apply principles from psychology to design products. Imagining users' reactions to an app's structure can be helpful. UX designers also interview potential users and conduct surveys to find out what potential consumers want (and don't want) from a product. This helps develop detailed profiles of imaginary users called personas. Each persona is created using information gathered from many different users. Personas help designers find a focus for design.

PHASE TWO: DESIGN

When research and structure planning are completed, engineers can then get started on the actual building of a website or app. At this point, UX designers have a good idea of who the audience for their product will be. The Three Principles of Vitruvius come into play during the design process. With a goal in place, designers can work on the information architecture of a site or app. UX designers then lay out a map of the entire user experience. Structure and content are planned from the first to the final user interaction. The pieces of the puzzle are arranged and connected to create a workable and enjoyable product.

WIREFRAMING

A wireframe is a blueprint for navigating through an app or site. Wireframes show what content will be used, where it will be presented, and how users can find it. Wireframes can simply be made with a pencil and a piece of paper or can be more in-depth with complex online tools. Most wireframes are free of pictures or images. The navigation and structure of the product need to be decided on first. Visual elements are added during the prototyping phase.

PROTOTYPING

A prototype is an early interactive rough draft that is produced before an app or site is built. Designers can decide how their product will best work and be most attractive to users. Prototyping can be simple or complex. It can be done with paper and pen or with specific software. The method used to create a prototype is not as important as the resulting prototype itself.

Prototypes are also helpful for product testing. Giving users a visual idea of what a product can accomplish lets a UX team know if they are on the right track. Prototyping saves both time and money. Since every step of the development process has been planned, prototypes give UX designers a chance to correct potential errors before they're included in a project. Features that may have made sense in wireframes may not work in a finished

Planning is an essential part of the design process. Mapping out the features and interface can prevent extra work during the coding of an app or other software.

product. Prototypes go through many iterations, or versions. Completed prototypes are shown to users to test the user interface.

PHASE THREE: BUILD AND INTEGRATE

Unlike the previous steps in the UX process, building an app or website is a collaborative effort. People with many different skills are needed to deliver a working product that will satisfy the needs of the project and delight users.

Once all of the pieces are in place, coding can begin. Although most UX engineers rarely code or build apps, they do need to understand HTML. Each one of the different platforms that will host an app or website has advantages and limitations for user experience interface. The UX designer's main focus during this phase is to keep aware of progress throughout the entire UX team.

UI design takes a front seat during this phase. A user's first impressions of a product can determine whether or not he or she will ever use it again. During this phase, the bones of the user interface (things like check boxes, menus, and buttons) are designed.

"Testing" would also be a good title for this phase. This is a trial-and-error process that involves finalizing layouts and images. As the website or app is built, errors found through testing are corrected before they make their way into the final product.

After the launch of an app, UX designers can track its usability and other metrics through focus groups, interviews, and user comments.

PHASE FOUR: THE LAUNCH & BEYOND

Even though a finished product is available to users, there's always room for improvement. Once a product is launched, UX engineers perform even more research. It's almost impossible to develop an app or website with no flaws right out of the gate. Now begins an ongoing process that involves identifying problems users may have after a launch and fixing them. In many cases, research may have to be repeated to make sure an issue is fully solved; it's rarely a one-time fix.

User testing after a launch is another way to judge how a product is doing. It's also an opportunity to make improvements. Users can be interviewed or given surveys, and their comments on social media may also be taken into account. A/B testing can also be done at this point. One group of users will be shown one version of an app or site and another group will see a second one. In some cases, multiple versions are used.

UX engineers also look at metrics, which measure how easy to use a product is. This data can be used to either fine-tune a site or app or make major changes. On a website, this includes:

» **Bounce rate**, which is the number of users who leave immediately after getting to a site;

» **Repeat visits**, or the number of users who return to a site; and

» **Conversion rate**, which accounts for the

Walt Disney: A UX Pioneer

Aside from creating cartoon legend Mickey Mouse, Walt Disney was also very concerned with enhancing the overall experience of his theme parks. The first to open, in 1955, was Disneyland Park in Anaheim, California. Disneyland helped set the standard for many theme parks today. In fact, many of the principles Disney used to design Disneyland and Disney World in Orlando, Florida, are very similar to the ideas behind the motives of UX engineers today.

Disney wanted his guests to have an immersive experience. Every interaction with visitors was planned, down to how the staff greeted visitors. Splitting up the park into several "worlds" that felt like separate theme parks gave visitors multiple choices. All of this was designed to make customers want to return and experience everything again.

The connection to UX may have been best demonstrated by the Experimental Prototype Community of Tomorrow, also known as EPCOT. At EPCOT, visitors had even more options. They could explore Future World or the World Showcase, a collection of eleven pavilions, each representing a different country. Disney called EPCOT a place "where the latest technology can be used to improve the lives of people." This sounds very close to the goals of UX and UI engineers.

Staff members on these projects were called imagineers. Disney also instructed his employees in the art of "plussing," or continually improving exhibits, even when they were deemed successful. This is a key aspect of UX design today.

Disney's UX experiments have worked quite well. More than seventeen million people pass through Disney World's

(Continued on the next page)

43

(Continued from the previous page)

gates each year. If that doesn't count as customer satisfaction, nothing does.

Walt Disney's amusement parks used modern technology, design, and psychology to make visitors' experiences enjoyable throughout their entire visit.

percentage of users who do things when they are on a site, such as providing an email address or signing up for a service or membership.

One of the metrics UX teams commonly analyze is trends on social media. There are some additional metrics that are considered for mobile apps.

The UX Toolbox

There are a few tools that the majority of UX engineers use to keep projects on time and organized. Deadline dates must be met, especially with so many people contributing to the launch of an app or website. Spreadsheets are common tools for UX engineers. This software is used for long-term planning, scheduling, and converting data into graphs and charts. Some UX designers use wireframing and prototyping programs. These professionals also need to be familiar with the graphic design software.

UX Formal Education

Very few schools offer specific undergraduate programs in UX design, but the number of them is growing. Since UX professionals draw experience from many areas, there are many different bachelor's degrees that one could earn to launch a career as a UX engineer. Computer science programs are a great place to start. Other degrees that would be helpful include information architecture, information science technology, and human-computer interaction. Some fine arts bachelor's degrees also offer concentrations in design and technology.

These program titles give a good idea of all of the different disciplines that are included in UX. At the graduate level, there are many more options for aspiring UX designers. The best way to find out if a program is right for you is to contact schools individually to see if they might be a good fit.

UX CERTIFICATIONS

The most specialized UX training is obtained through certification programs. Certification has some great benefits. For one, these programs are much cheaper than four-year college programs. They also take less time to complete. Some range from a few weekends to full-time classes for ten or more weeks, with tuition ranging anywhere from a few thousand dollars to around $20,000. Many companies select UX employees based on them having achieved certification.

There is a drawback to certification programs. Many don't accept students without bachelor degrees. Having a degree regardless of whether or not a person has obtained the specific UX skills needed makes it easier to enter the world of UX.

UX Job Outlook and Salary

Over the past few years, more companies have increasingly concentrated on design in their products. Consequently, the future looks very bright for those wanting to enter this profession. User experience designers are in demand, and this need looks to increase.

The United States Bureau of Labor Statistics doesn't currently have specific statistics for UX engineers, but jobs for web development professionals are expected to increase by about 25 percent by 2025. According to the salary information company PayScale, the median salary for UX designers is much higher than the average for other jobs. Experience and skills can raise salaries as well.

CHAPTER FIVE

UI ENGINEERS: THE JOB

A UI designer takes the path laid out by the UX design team and helps to flesh it out. User interface designers are responsible for content; while they may not write all of it, they're responsible for its presentation. The UI process requires skills in visual design, digital illustration, and motion graphics.

Graphic design deals with printed materials; visual design is its digital companion. The latter involves crafting and changing static images for sites and apps. While visual design focuses on the overall look and presentation of a website or app, interaction design covers what happens when and after a user makes a decision or choice. Pulling down on a touchscreen to refresh a page with new information is a great example.

Interaction design includes so much: menus, error messages, pop-ups, alerts, and warnings. These parts of user interfaces are called elements. The placement of these elements should look the same throughout a product.

Microinteractions

Microinteractions are exactly what they sound like—small, one-time interactions between a user and a device. Microinteractions are all around us. Whenever users swipe to accomplish a goal, "like" something on social media, set an alarm, or even simply turn on a device's on/off switch, they are coming face-to-face with a microinteraction. Great microinteractions usually consist of one simple movement, not a combination of gestures.

When added up, all of these small moments create a large part of a user's experience, making it as smooth and as natural as possible.

Users can have dozens of microinteractions with devices when performing tasks such as logging in, controlling value, and viewing photos.

Details are important, but microinteractions should not be used to show off. Remember, invisible design works best! They should be so natural to a user that he or she doesn't notice that they're even occurring. Microinteractions are all around us. Great microinteractions usually consist of one simple movement, not a combination of gestures. All of these perfect little moments add up, so each one should be as smooth and as natural as possible.

Also, since animation is a big part of websites and apps, interaction design requires a good knowledge of motion design. The animated transitions from screen to screen should be uniform throughout different platforms as well.

THE UI TOOLBOX

Some of the tools UI engineers use include:
- » **Pen and paper.** This is the original computer. Great UI design can often start from the simplest doodles and sketches.
- » **Photo editing software.** Programs such as Adobe Photoshop are great for working with existing images or photos, although they are not the best choice for creating images.
- » **Vector graphics editing.** Vector graphics are used to create original images, such as corporate and brand logos. They're very useful for UI designers, especially when creating page layouts and typography. These programs include Adobe Illustrator, Fireworks, and Sketch.
- » **Motion graphics software.** Motion graphics animate things on a site or app. The moving elements of an app or site are what makes them enjoyable to use.

Skeuomorphics

Skeuomorphism is very common in the world of UI. The term is used when objects in the digital world resemble physical objects. Skeuomorphics are features that are not immediately noticeable in apps or software. Aside from looking good, they give users an idea of what they can do within an application.

Modern computers are more user-friendly than ever before thanks to skeuomorphic icons and apps that help navigate and understand applications.

Digital clocks that look like real watches or magazine apps that allow a person to choose from a library-style rack fit this model. The sound of a shutter click when using a phone to take a picture and an address book app that opens like a real book are also skeuomorphics. Even the basic look of a desktop on a computer is skeuomorphic. It resembles a real office, with folders and files and helps keep our digital world organized, and it even has a trash can for digital garbage.

The release of the iPhone brought a great deal of attention to skeuomorphic design. Before then, websites were more concerned with creating new graphic elements in the digital world rather than imitating the real. Today, skeuomorphic design is still evolving. The shiny, glossy buttons of the last decade have given way to a simpler flat design with less reflection. Most likely, design trends will be different in the future, as skeuomorphics tend to change with tastes and trends outside of digital design.

FORMAL DEGREES AND CERTIFICATION

UI programs are becoming more common, with more at the bachelor level now than ever before. Some use the term "user interface," but programs such as media and interaction design, interactive media, and industrial design all contain coursework that would help hopeful UI engineers enter the profession.

A degree in information technology or information architecture would be helpful, also. Mixing a degree in either of these disciplines with courses in fine arts (or vice versa) is another way to get a solid skill set for the job market.

Many of the schools and institutes that offer UX certifications also do the same for UI design. As is the case with UX certification, many UI certification programs require a bachelor's degree for admission. Another option would be to learn visual design, motion graphics, and other skills necessary for UI at a university and then enroll in a certification program.

Aside from formal schooling, there are many ways to learn IT skills today. More and more companies are hiring IT people who may not have college diplomas. A college degree will still give the most options, but it's good to know that success in IT is not always dependent upon a four-year university pathway. Many companies still require certain certifications of their new hires, but ability and skills can go a long way, especially in UX and UI.

EARLY EDUCATION

There are plenty of opportunities to learn about UX and UI design even before attending college is considered. Some have been around for years while others are relatively new, but all of them can be helpful on a person's journey to becoming a UX or UI engineer.

HACKATHONS

Hackathons are participatory events that involve problem solving, collaboration, and quick thinking. Several branches of technology have a hackathon geared for them or attached to them. During a hackathon, a goal of some sort is always set by those people who run the event. Some goals are very specific ("use our software to build an innovative camera app"), while some are very broad ("using Java, create a brand new app"). No matter what, hackathons require creativity and a touch of innovation. They also offer the opportunity to meet other aspiring coders and creative people who want to be at the forefront of the tech revolution.

Every hackathon has its own rules for participation, so some investigation is typically necessary to find a good fit. Some may be more for people with experience, while others encourage and welcome newbies who want to learn. Many hackathons are free, and the ones that aren't

Working efficiently as a team under a deadline is necessary for UX and UI designers. Hackathon participants rely on many of the same skills when solving problems at events.

usually have a low admission fee. Some hackathons have an age limit, but many do not. Sites such as Eventbrite have extensive listings of the hackathons in a given area. Looking for them on any search engine will yield plenty of results as well.

MENTORSHIPS

If you'd prefer to work one-on-one with someone as you learn the ins and outs of UX, you may want to consider a mentorship. A mentor is someone who can provide support and advice in a field of study. Many people with skills in a profession love to share what they know with younger people. One word of advice: be prepared! Those seeking a mentor should have a focus in mind before beginning their search. Specific questions are great. Mentors do not simply teach; they interact with their mentees. Anyone interested in UX or UI should learn what he or she can and then find guidance. A good mentorship relies on participation from both sides.

There are a few ways to find a mentor. Attending a hackathon is a great way to start. While there probably won't be mentors actively looking for people to help, these individuals may be found through asking around, observation, and participation. Attendance at a UX or UI meetup also can help in a mentor search.

DIGITAL RELATIONSHIPS

Social media, blogs, and forums are excellent resources for getting a basic knowledge of a subject. Find people whose work is appealing online and watch their blogs or follow them on social media. It's a great way to keep informed about what they're working on. These people may be open to being contacted for questions or advice.

WORKING ON YOUR OWN

What else can a prospective UX or UI engineer do before becoming a member of the workforce? Plenty. Some schools, libraries, computer shops, and makerspaces offer free or low-cost classes in coding or computer design. There are also plenty of free online resources that teach the fundamentals of UX and UI. Reading about the field is another way to expand one's knowledge. There are thousands of books that teach UX and UI skills. A few of them are listed in the back of this book.

Learning how to use the software that UX and UI engineers rely on can also provide an advantage when it's time to look at college or online programs. At a minimum, a good foundation could make the next phase of a person's education easier.

Copying is also a great tool. Looking at other UX and UI projects to see how they work is a great way to learn. This is called deconstruction or reverse engineering.

Taking a design apart to see how the parts fit together can be highly educational. Future UX and UI engineers should be careful not to plagiarize the work of others, meaning not to copy so closely that it is stealing.

Like users, UX and UI engineers need to feel engaged when they work. Those who want to become UX and UI engineers need to consider which sites and apps they regularly use and enjoy, and start by studying them.

UI Job Outlook and Salary

The United States Bureau of Labor Statistics doesn't list specific information for UI engineers, but the need for web development professionals looks to increase by about 25 percent over the next ten years. Glassdoor, a site that gets its salary information from employees, estimates the average salary for a user interface engineer to be more than the US median income. Depending on the company, starting salaries can sometimes be higher. Apps and software reach a global audience and generate billions of dollars a year. High pay for these positions is to be expected.

CHAPTER SIX

FUTURE DIRECTIONS FOR INTERACTION

It's completely possible that in fifteen years another technology will become more popular than the smartphone. By looking at some products that are already in the marketplace, some educated guesses can be made as to what the future may hold. Why mention this here? Because these devices will all need great UX and UI to both work and keep users engaged. The more technology improves, the more the world will need talented UX and UI designers to make it easy to use and understand.

THE INTERNET OF THINGS

All of the information on the internet is user-generated. At some point, a human being wrote the code that runs a site or the site's text. Smart technology is quickly changing the balance and shifting more responsibility to our devices. Together, they make up what has been called the Internet of Things. This term is used to talk about smart devices or connected devices. In the past, computers could only do what they were programmed to do. In the twenty-first century and beyond, computers will obtain data from users, then use that information to perform tasks so that people don't have to. For instance, computers can crunch numbers and process data much better than humans. As consumer expert Kevin Ashton once said:

> If we had computers that knew everything there was to know about things—using data they gathered without any help from us—we would be able to track and count everything, and greatly reduce waste, loss, and cost. We would know when things needed replacing, repairing or recalling, and whether they were fresh or past their best.

The Internet of Things will continue to build on things that already exist and give them more information and control over what they can do. For example, the GPS in most smartphones may one day be used to navigate self-driving cars.

Even without human beings to collect data, UX and UI designers will still be needed to create interfaces and experiences. These future interfaces will be more complex because the tech behind them is more complicated. Moving from the physical world to the digital world and back presents new challenges. More devices than ever will be connected, and designers may have to develop new strategies to harness them all.

Gesture Technology

Gesture recognition is all around, especially in phones and video games. The finger movements used to control today's phones are all gestures. Fingers are used in the same way that people used the first mouse with the Xerox Alto. The motion-sensing cameras, sensors, and remote controls that have deepened our gaming experiences are gesture based, too.

Voice activation has moved inside our vehicles and enabled the design of driverless cars and other systems that use voice recognition.

The applications of gesture recognition are endless. In the future, the medical industry will benefit from gesture technology. Imagine a doctor being able to access patient records with a wave of his or her hand. One day, gesture-controlled robots could administer medicine or assist in surgery.

VOICE ACTIVATION

Like gesture technology, many people use voice activation every day. It's become even more common since the release of both Siri, Apple's digital assistant, and Amazon Echo's Alexa. Both not only obey commands and let users control media and order things, but they also respond in full sentences. These virtual helpers will eventually appear in most homes and many workspaces where hands-free communication is preferred.

These devices are getting better and smarter every day, but the technology has not been perfected. In the

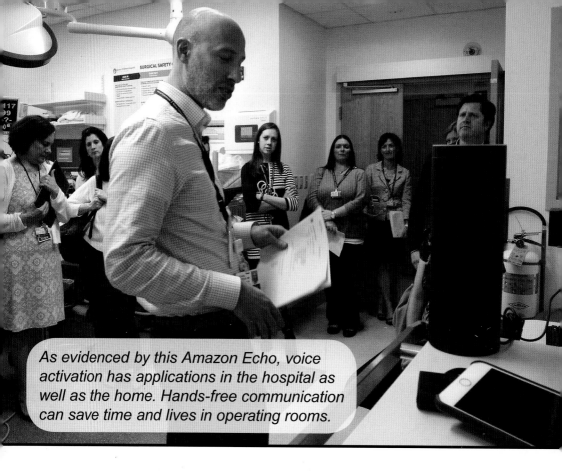

As evidenced by this Amazon Echo, voice activation has applications in the hospital as well as the home. Hands-free communication can save time and lives in operating rooms.

physical world, mistakes are not as easy to fix as in the digital one. These devices still need to be programmed by humans. This is why many companies are spending millions of dollar on artificial intelligence to tackle this problem. However, these modern devices are much more sophisticated than those from the early days of voice recognition technology, and prospects are very encouraging.

AUGMENTED AND VIRTUAL REALITY

Although augmented reality (AR) has been around since the 1990s, the technology has continued to develop. AR adds sounds and images to one's normal perception of reality. In other words, augmented reality improves the physical world by placing digital enhancements on top of it. Some of the most well-known AR devices in use today are smart glasses. Using digital overlays, they allow users to make phone calls, get directions, take pictures, and monitor their health. Eventually, augmented reality devices may enhance smartphones or possibly replace them.

Augmented reality (AR) can make digital experiences more immersive by adding a digital layer to the physical world. AR is used in gaming and other smart technology, like Pokémon Go.

Virtual reality takes augmented reality to the next level. Instead of enhancing the world around us, virtual reality creates a separate world with which users can interact. As with augmented reality, VR has been in development for more than thirty years. Though the original devices used were clunky and awkward, virtual reality interfaces have become much smoother. In the future, people may be able to climb Mount Everest or walk with dinosaurs from the safety of their living rooms.

Virtual reality can't be used while walking down a busy street; it requires complete immersion in whatever world the user has decided to explore. Up until now, the technology has mostly developed through video gaming, but some new smartphones are taking advantage of the technology. Aside from entertainment, virtual reality will most likely change the way people take classes, work, shop, and live.

Wearables and Bio-integration

Wearable devices are already impacting the public's lives. People use them to monitor their health and track physical activity. Wearable tech also allows users to communicate with both human beings and other devices. The world of wearables is also connected to the Internet of Things. The sensors and software that gather and process data don't need much input once they're programmed.

Two big recent advances in this space have been battery life and size. In terms of UX and UI, users want almost invisible wearables that don't have to be recharged daily. Some new sensors are thinner and bendable, which will enable users to wear these devices directly on their skin like Band-Aids. The next generation of fabrics will have sensors woven directly into them. One day, clothing will be able to collect information about its wearer and help him or her live a healthier life. These advances may make the next generation of wearables as common as smartphones.

Zero UI Is the Future

Many people could not imagine life without a smartphone. These devices help them live their lives on the go. However, current research indicates that it is possible to live "screenless" lives one day. That's right—one day the "swipe" people have come to know and love will most likely become obsolete. To quote Google CEO Sundar Pichai, "Looking to the future, the next big step will be for the very concept of the 'device' to go away." One day, it will be possible to use digital devices without a thought. Although this seems like something out of the latest summer sci-fi blockbuster, it's much closer to reality than may be realized. This new frontier is called zero UI.

Devices are becoming much better at understanding complex language and gestures. They can "learn" habits and schedules and make educated guesses about a person's likes, dislikes, and choices. Technology is taking humankind on a path toward zero UI. It will mean less time spent in front of computers while accomplishing the same tasks. Who wouldn't like more time to engage with the physical world?

People live in a digital society. In a consumer-driven culture, they are always on the hunt for digital experiences that are entertaining, educational, informative, and useful. Applications on smartphones, tablets, computers, and televisions have gone from being simply entertaining to helping users live healthier and more organized lives. Furthermore, technology is improving on a daily basis and shows little signs of declining in the future. As more digital platforms and systems develop, the world will need more specialists to understand the best ways to interface with them in the most natural and realistic ways.

Working in UX or UI is a great way to be at the cutting edge of this revolution. Anyone who enjoys projects that require organization, teamwork, and problem solving should consider looking at a career in user experience. For those curious about the world of UX but who want to include art and visual design, then exploring user interaction may be a better option. The future job prospects for these professions is well above average and will remain so far into the future.

Glossary

BANDWIDTH The amount or speed of data that can be transmitted in a certain amount of time.

DATA Gathered information.

DEVELOPER A writer of computer programs or web applications.

FEEDBACK Information gathered regarding users' reactions to a product.

FOCUS GROUP A group of people from whom tech professionals can get feedback on how a product works for users.

FUNCTIONALITY What can be accomplished by a particular application or website.

GRAPHIC DESIGN A profession or skill that uses fonts, images, logos, and other graphic techniques to create a look or identity for a brand or idea.

GRAPHICS USER INTERFACE (GUI) A way for users to interact with a computer or electronic device.

IMMERSIVE Completely engaging.

INTERFACE To interact or communicate.

ITERATIVE DESIGN Product design that relies on revising multiple times after user feedback.

LAUNCH To release an application or software to the public.

MICROINTERACTION A single interaction between a user and device to accomplish one small goal.

NETWORK A group of linked computers or devices.

PLATFORM A programming tool used by a developer to build an application.

PROTOTYPE An early, often incomplete version of a product.

RESOLUTION The number of pixels on a digital screen. The more pixels, the better the picture.

SERVER A computer or computers that connect the users in a network.

USER INTERFACE The way in which humans interact with computers to both input and receive information.

USER EXPERIENCE The overall experience a person has when using a product.

WIREFRAME An early and basic design of structure and organization for a website or application.

FOR MORE INFORMATION

Awwwards

Awards Online S.L.
C/ Crevillente, 10-15a
Valencia 46022
Spain
Email: awwwards@awwwards.com
Website: http://www.awwwards.com
Awwwards recognizes the talent and effort of the best web designers, developers, and agencies in the world. Recent winners have developed mobile apps for Hewlett-Packard, Converse, and Vimeo.

BrainStation

460 King Street W
Toronto, ON M5V 1K7
Canada
(800) 903-5159
Email: contact@brainstation.io
Website: https://brainstation.io
BrainStation is a collective of coders and other creative people that provides training in all aspects of product development from coding to UX and UI design to marketing.

CanUX

37 Fairpark Drive
Ottowa, ON K2G 6X8
Canada
(613) 864-3020
Email: info@canux.io
Website: http://canux.io

CanUX is the largest annual UX event in Canada. It's organized and run by volunteers and runs for three days. Experts in various fields give lectures on topics including UX, UI, and information design.

Meetup, Inc.
632 Broadway, 10th Floor
New York, NY 10012
(212) 225-7327
Email: support@meetup.com
Website: https://www.meetup.com
Meetup.com helps people all over the world connect based on activities and ideas, including UX and UI engineers.

Nielsen Norman Group
48105 Warm Springs Boulevard
Fremont, CA 94539-7498
(415) 685-4230
Email: info@nngroup.com
Website: https://www.nngroup.com
Nielsen Norman Group specializes in evidence-based user experience research, training, and consulting. It offers free downloadable reports on UX and other resources.

United States Department of Education Office of Career, Technical, and Adult Education (OCTAE)
Division of Academic and Technical Education
400 Maryland Avenue SW
Washington, DC 20202-7100
(202) 245-7700

Email: octae@ed.gov
Website: http://sites.ed.gov/octae
OCTAE is an office of the US government that manages programs and grants that help give young people skills for high-skill, high-wage, or high-demand occupations in the twenty-first century global economy.

Usability.gov

US Department of Health and Human Services
Digital Communications Division
200 Independence Avenue SW
Washington, DC 20201
(202) 604-7925
Email: info.usability@hhs.gov
Website: https://www.usability.gov/
Usability.gov is a government-run UX and UI resource for both students and professionals.

WEBSITES

Because of the changing nature of internet links, Rosen Publishing has developed an online list of websites related to the subject of this book. This site is updated regularly. Please use this link to access the list:

http://www.rosenlinks.com/TECHT/UX

FOR FURTHER READING

Banga, Cameron, and Josh Weinhold. *Essential Mobile Interaction Design: Perfecting Interface Design in Mobile Apps* (Usability). Boston, MA: Addison-Wesley Professional, 2014.

Clinton, Steve. *Apps: Beginner's Guide for App Programming, App Development, App Design.* 2nd ed. Charleston, SC: CreateSpace Independent Publishing Platform, 2015.

Cooper, Alan, Robert Reimann, David Cronin, and Christophen Noessel. *About Face: The Essentials of Interaction Design.* 4th ed.. Hoboken, NJ: John Wiley & Sons, 2014.

Eyal, Nir. *Hooked: How to Build Habit-Forming Products.* New York, NY: Portfolio, 2014.

Henry, Scott. *Drawing for Product Designers.* (Portfolio Skills: Product Design). London, UK: Laurence King Publishing, 2012.

Lal, Rajesh. *Digital Design Essentials: 100 Ways to Design Better Desktop, Web, and Mobile Interfaces.* London, UK: Rockport Publishers, 2013.

McKay, Everett N. *UI Is Communication: How to Design Intuitive, User Centered Interfaces by Focusing on Effective Communication.* Burlington, MA: Morgan Kauffman, 2013.

Neil, Theresa. *Mobile Design Pattern Gallery: UI Patterns for Smartphone Apps.* Sebastopol, CA: O'Reilly Media, 2014.

Shedroff, Nathan, and Christopher Noessel. *Make It So: Design Lessons from Science Fiction.* Brooklyn, NY: Rosenfeld Media, 2012.

Tidwell, Jenifer. *Designing Interfaces: Patterns for Effective Interaction Design.* 2nd ed. Sebastopol, CA: O'Reilly Media, 2011.

Unger, Russ, and Carolyn Chandler. *LA Project Guide to UX Design: For User Experience Designers in the Field or in the Making.* Sebastopol, CA: O'Reilly Media, 2013.

Williams, Robin. *The Non-Designer's Design Book.* 4th ed. San Francisco, CA: Peachpit Press, 2014.

BIBLIOGRAPHY

Bruni, Ezequiel. "The Beginner's Guide to UX Prototyping." Webdesigner Depot RSS, April 4, 2016. http://www. webdesignerdepot.com/2016/04/the -beginners-guide-to-ux-prototyping/.

Dickerson, Joseph. "Walt Disney: The World's First UX Designer." UX Magazine, September 9, 2013. https:// uxmag.com/articles/walt-disney-the-worlds-first-ux -designer.

Eugenios, Jillian. "Best Jobs in America." CNN, January 27, 2015. http://money.cnn.com/gallery/pf/2015/01/27 /best-jobs-2015/14.html.

Garrett, Jesse James. *The Elements of User Experience: User-Centered Design for the Web and Beyond* (Voices That Matter). 2nd Edition. San Francisco, CA: New Riders, 2010.

Krug, Steve. *Don't Make Me Think: A Common Sense Approach to Web Usability* (Voices That Matter). 2nd Edition. San Francisco, CA: New Riders, 2005.

Lamprecht, Emil. "The Difference Between UX and UI Design: A Layman's Guide." Accessed October 10, 2016. http://blog.careerfoundry.com/ui-design/the -difference-between-ux-and-ui-design-a-laymans -guide/.

Ming, Lo Min. "UI, UX: Who Does What? A Designer's Guide to the Tech Industry." Co.Design, August 16, 2016. https://www.fastcodesign .com/3032719/ui-ux-who-does-what-a-designers -guide-to-the-tech-industry.

Nielsen, Jakob. "Usability 101: Introduction to Usability." January 12, 2012. https://www.nngroup.com/articles /usability-101-introduction-to-usability/.

Norman, Donald A. *The Design of Everyday Things*. New York, NY: Basic Books, 2002.

Rutherford, Zack. "6 Examples of Awful UX Design." September 29, 2015. http://thenextweb.com /dd/2015/09/29/6-examples-of-awful-ux-design/#gref.

Safer, Dan. *Microinteractions: Full Color Edition: Designing with Details*. Sebastopol, CA: O'Reilly Media, 2013.

"Salary: User Experience Designer." September 22, 2016. https://www.glassdoor.com/Salaries/user -experience-designer-salary-SRCH_KO0,24.htm.

"Salary: User Interface Designer." Accessed October 30, 2016. https://www.glassdoor.com/Salaries/user -interface-designer-salary-SRCH_KO0,23.htm.

US Deptartment of Health and Human Services. *The Research-Based Web Design & Usability Guidelines*. Enlarged/Expanded edition. Washington, DC: US Government Printing Office, 2006.

"Web Developers: Occupational Outlook Handbook: US Bureau of Labor Statistics," December 17, 2015, http:// www.bls.gov/ooh/computer-and-information -technology/web-developers.htm.

INDEX

A

Advanced Research Projects
    Agency Network, 26
Alexa (Amazon Echo), 61
Alto Workstation, 31, 60
animation, 50
artificial intelligence, 62
Ashton, Kevin, 59
augmented reality (AR), 62–64

B

Berners-Lee, Tim, 27, 28
bounce rate, 42
browsers, 35
  origins of, 28–29
  static, 28
Bureau of Labor Statistics, 47, 57
buttons, problem of small, 33

C

coding, 13, 19, 27, 29, 40, 56, 58
content strategy, 17
conversion rate, 42–45
customer satisfaction, 4, 19, 23

D

data
  big data, 13
  definition, 9
  managing, 13–15
  organization, 11
database administrators, 13
data engineers, 13, 15
deconstruction, 56–57
design, 37–40
digital assistants, 61–62
Disney, Walt, and UX, 43–44

E

efficiency, 22
elements, 48
EPCOT, 43

F

fingers, use of, 34
Flash, 32
focus groups, 7
front-end designers, 19, 29
functionality, 17

G

gestures and gesture technology,
  49, 60–61
graphical user interface (GUI),
  12, 31, 34
graphic design, 48

ABOUT THE AUTHOR

Kerry Hinton has been a full-fledged participant in the digital revolution since he learned to program on an Atari 800. After winning the Golden Disk Award at computer camp, he became convinced that computers were the future and never looked back. Over the past twenty years, he's moved from Macs to PCs to Macs to tablets and everywhere in between. He lives in Hoboken, New Jersey, and spends a little too much time reading about and working with computers.

PHOTO CREDITS: